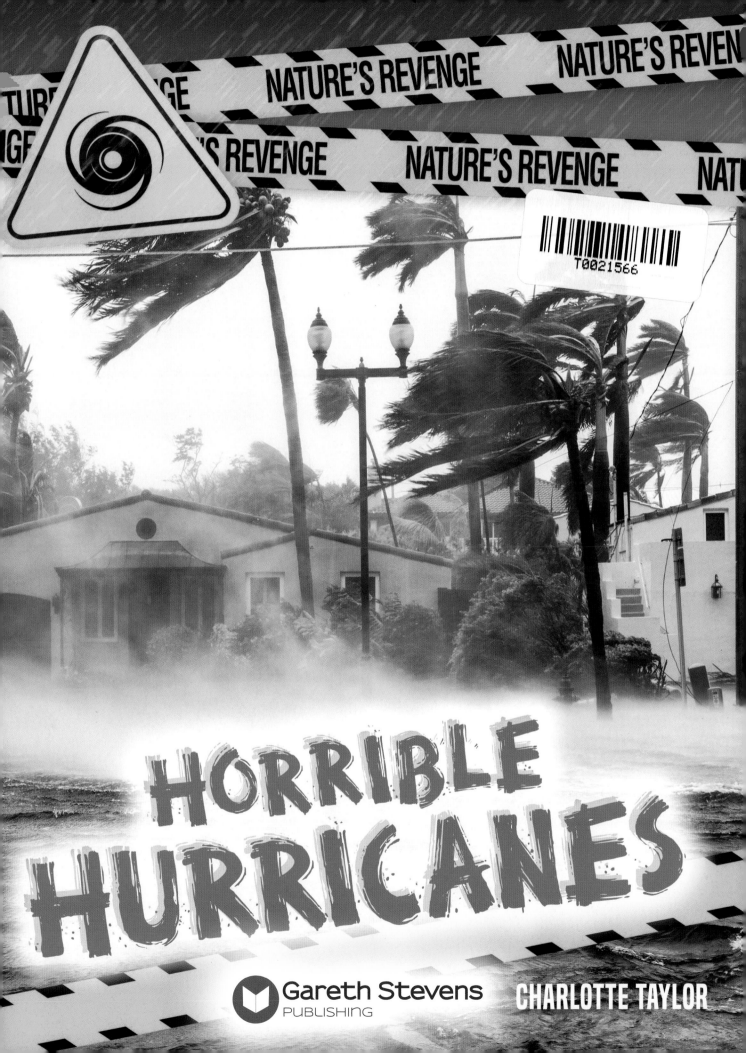

NATURE'S REVENGE

NATURE'S REVENGE

T0021566

HORRIBLE HURRICANES

Gareth Stevens
PUBLISHING

CHARLOTTE TAYLOR

Please visit our website, www.garethstevens.com. For a free color catalog of all our high-quality books, call toll free 1-800-542-2595 or fax 1-877-542-2596.

Cataloging-in-Publication Data
Names: Taylor, Charlotte, 1978-.
Title: Horrible hurricanes / Charlotte Taylor.
Description: New York : Gareth Stevens Publishing, 2023. | Series: Nature's revenge | Includes glossary and index.
Identifiers: ISBN 9781538280478 (pbk.) | ISBN 9781538280492 (library bound) | ISBN 9781538280485 (6pack) | ISBN 9781538280508 (ebook)
Subjects: LCSH: Hurricanes–Juvenile literature. | Natural disasters–Juvenile literature.
Classification: LCC QC944.2 T39 2023 | DDC 551.55'2–dc23

Portions of this work were originally authored by Melissa Raé Shofner and published as *Hammered by Hurricanes*. All new material in this edition was authored by Charlotte Taylor.

Published in 2023 by
Gareth Stevens Publishing
29 East 21st Street
New York, NY 10010

Designer: Leslie Taylor
Editor: Megan Quick

Photo credits: Cover, p. 1 FotoKina/Shutterstock.com; pp. 1–32 (icons-series artwork) Vector by/Shutterstock.com; pp. 1–32 (hazard tape-series artwork) DDevecee/Shutterstock.com; p. 4 (sign) Chuck Wagner/Shutterstock.com; p. 5 Mia2you/Shutterstock.com; p. 7 Designua/Shutterstock.com; p. 9 https://en.wikipedia.org/wiki/File:Staring_Down_Hurricane_Florence.jpg; p. 11 https://commons.wikimedia.org/wiki/File:Cityscape_of_Taipei_Taiwan_during_typhoon_2015.jpg; p. 13 FEMA/Alamy.com; p. 14 kckate16 Shutterstock.com; p. 15 Jeffrey Isaac Greenberg 12+/Alamy.com; p. 17 https://commons.wikimedia.org/wiki/File:01E_2016_5day.gif; p. 19 Lisa F. Young/Shutterstock.com; p. 21 https://commons.wikimedia.org/wiki/File:Empty_supermarket_shelves_before_Hurricane_Sandy,_Montgomery,_NY.jpg; p. 23 https://scijinks.gov/hurricane/cyclone_map_large.png; p. 25 https://commons.wikimedia.org/wiki/File:Damage_to_New_Jersey_shore_amusement_park_(8151149663).jpg; p. 27 BlueRingMedia/Shutterstock.com; p. 29 michelmond/Shutterstock.com.

Printed in the United States of America

Some of the images in this book illustrate individuals who are models. The depictions do not imply actual situations or events.

CPSIA compliance information: Batch #CSGS23: For further information contact Gareth Stevens, New York, New York at 1-800-542-2595.

Find us on

CONTENTS

Words in the glossary appear in **bold** type the first time they are used in the text.

SERIOUS STORMS

Hurricanes are some of the most dangerous storms in the world. High winds, heavy rainfall, and serious flooding leave **damage** and death in their path. Hurricanes can stretch over hundreds of miles and affect large areas. It's not unusual for hurricanes to produce one or more tornadoes. And, believe it or not, many scientists believe hurricanes are going to get even more **intense**.

An area's weather over a long period of time is called its climate. Earth's climate is changing, partly because of human activities. This is causing lots of problems for our planet. One of these problems is **extreme** weather. And weather doesn't get more extreme than a hurricane!

Local businesses board up windows to prepare for Hurricane Irma in 2017.

High winds from Hurricane Irma slammed the coast of Florida in 2017.

The ABCs of Hurricane Names

You may have noticed that hurricanes have people's names. Naming storms began in 1953 as a quick and easy way to identify them. For Atlantic Ocean storms, there are six alphabetical lists of 24 names (no Q or U) that are reused every six years. If a storm is very deadly or costly, the name is removed from the list and replaced by another name so it isn't used again.

A HURRICANE FORMS

Hurricanes start near the **equator**, where waters are very warm. When winds move over the ocean, the water evaporates, turning from liquid to water **vapor**. The vapor rises and cools, forming tall clouds and large raindrops. This rising warm air creates a low-pressure area near the ocean's surface. Cool air pushes in to replace it, then warms and rises as well.

Sometimes, the air around the low-pressure area begins to move in a fast **spiral**. Warm, wet ocean air continues to be sucked up and carried out and over the storm, which causes wind speeds to increase. Faster winds create lower air pressure at the center of the storm, and the pattern continues.

A Closer Look at Air Pressure

Air pressure can be high or low. High pressure usually means fair weather, while low-pressure systems often create storms. Air pressure comes from the gases in the atmosphere. You don't feel it, but air actually weighs 14.7 pounds per square inch. When an area has low pressure, winds naturally flow toward it and then rise. The rising air cools and forms clouds.

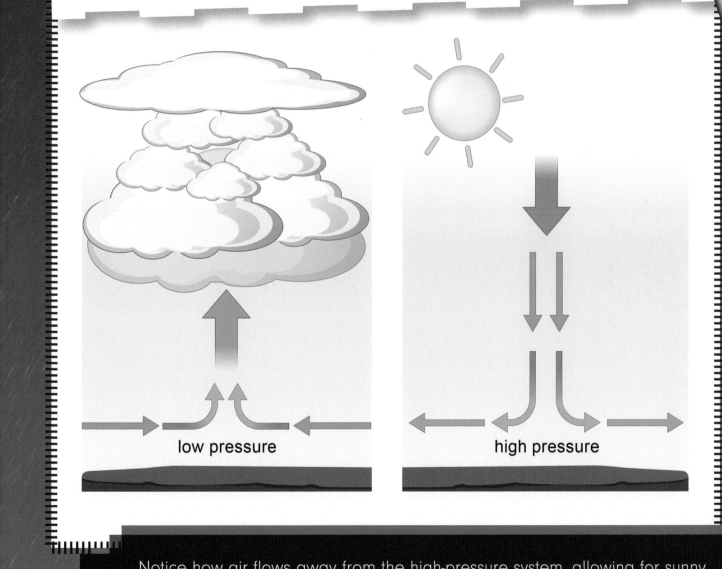

low pressure

high pressure

Notice how air flows away from the high-pressure system, allowing for sunny weather. Air flows toward the low-pressure system, forming clouds and rain.

CENTER OF THE STORM

Every hurricane has a center. This is the area of low pressure where the storm begins, and it is called the eye. As winds increase, they spin around the eye. Unlike the rest of the storm, the air within the eye of a hurricane is calm and cloudless.

If you are ever in a hurricane, don't be fooled by the calm conditions in the eye of the storm. The most dangerous part of the hurricane—the eyewall—will hit again soon. As its name suggests, the eyewall of a hurricane surrounds the eye. The strongest winds and heaviest rains are found here.

Rainbands

Rainbands are responsible for bursts of heavy rain and strong winds in a hurricane. These long, curved bands of thunderstorm clouds spiral away from the eye of the hurricane. Between bands, there are periods of calmer weather. As you move farther out from the eye, the intensity of wind and rain decreases.

An image taken from space clearly shows the eye of Hurricane Florence, which hit North and South Carolina in 2018.

THE HURRICANE GROWS

A storm goes through several stages before it becomes a hurricane. It starts out as a **tropical** disturbance. This occurs when clouds begin to organize and show a slight spinning motion. If this continues, the storm may become a tropical depression. Tropical depressions have wind speeds between 25 and 38 miles (40.2 and 61.2 km) per hour.

If the system keeps getting stronger, it may become a tropical storm, with wind speeds from 39 to 73 miles (62.8 to 117.5 km) per hour. At this stage, winds begin to swirl around a developed eye, and the storm is given a name. When wind speeds top 74 miles (119.1 km) per hour, the storm is considered a hurricane.

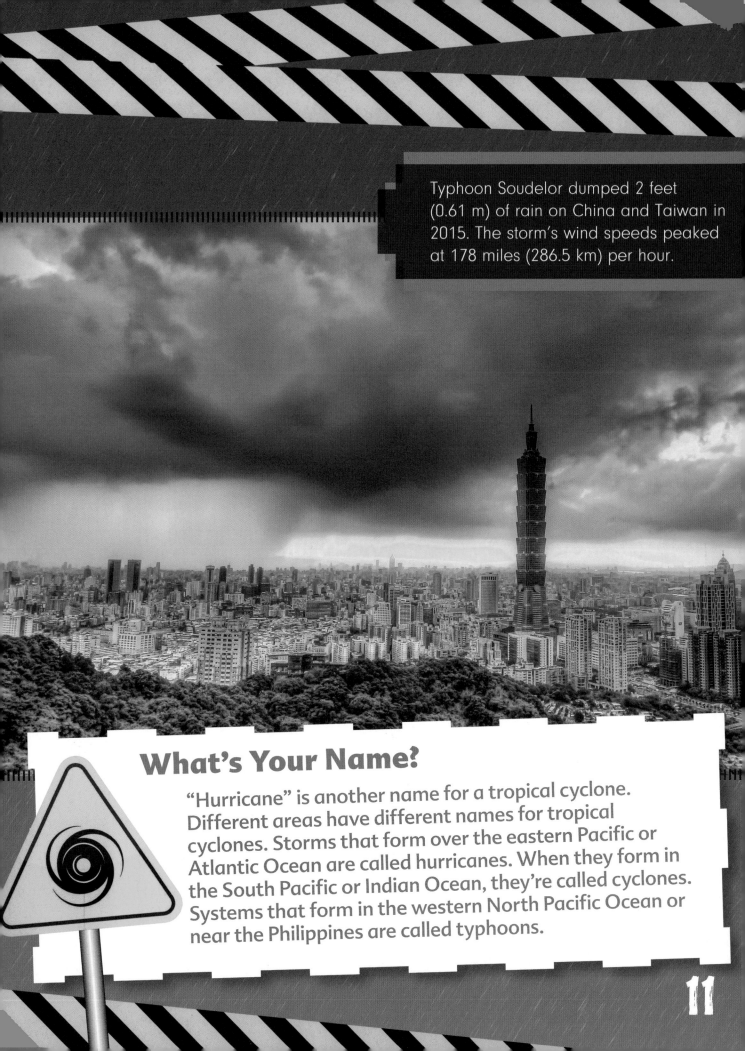

Typhoon Soudelor dumped 2 feet (0.61 m) of rain on China and Taiwan in 2015. The storm's wind speeds peaked at 178 miles (286.5 km) per hour.

What's Your Name?

"Hurricane" is another name for a tropical cyclone. Different areas have different names for tropical cyclones. Storms that form over the eastern Pacific or Atlantic Ocean are called hurricanes. When they form in the South Pacific or Indian Ocean, they're called cyclones. Systems that form in the western North Pacific Ocean or near the Philippines are called typhoons.

WIND AND WATER

All hurricanes are dangerous, but some are more dangerous than others. Scientists measure each hurricane to figure out how powerful it is. They study wind speeds as well as the possible storm surge, which is when seawater rises and is pushed onto the land by strong winds. A storm surge may be as high as 20 feet (6.1 m), which means flooding is a huge danger.

Hurricane winds can be very damaging, but it's the water that is the most deadly part of the storm. Over nearly 50 years, about 88 percent of deaths in the United States from tropical depressions, tropical storms, and hurricanes were water related. High surf, storm surges, and flooding due to rainfall can spell disaster.

Residents wait to be rescued from their rooftops after Hurricane Katrina caused major flooding in New Orleans, Louisiana, in 2005.

Storm Rankings

The Saffir-Simpson scale is a special system used to rank hurricanes. The scale places hurricanes into five categories based on top wind speed and possible property damage. Category 1 hurricanes have lower winds, while Category 5 hurricanes are often **catastrophic**. Any storm that is Category 3 or higher is considered a major hurricane.

HIGH-TECH FORECASTS

Being prepared for a hurricane saves lives, so it's important to know when a big storm is on its way. Meteorologists are scientists who study weather, climate, and the atmosphere. It is their job to **forecast** the path of a hurricane long before it makes landfall. They use modern technology to make faster, more precise hurricane **predictions**. This means warnings can be issued sooner.

Weather **satellites** can provide a view of Earth from space. They allow meteorologists to view changes in clouds that can show the formation of a hurricane as well as its strength. People can also use satellite images to track a hurricane's path and make predictions about where it will make landfall.

Drones are equipped with cameras that give important information to track storms.

A meteorologist will use computer technology to track a storm.

NATIONAL HURRICANE CENTER
TROPICAL PREDICTION CENTER
AT FLORIDA INTERNATIONAL UNIVERSITY

Hurricane Drones

For many years, people have flown planes called Hurricane Hunters into storms to gather information like wind speed and air pressure. Now scientists have a new flying tool: drones. The unmanned machines can get closer to the ocean's surface than planes and get more accurate, or correct, measurements of the storm. Scientists hope the drones will help them understand hurricanes better and save lives.

15

WATCHES AND WARNINGS

The National Hurricane Center (NHC) warns people when a hurricane is heading toward them. If scientists believe an area may experience hurricane conditions within 36 hours, they issue a hurricane watch. Meteorologists use computer models and other methods to make a "best track" forecast. This is their best guess about where a hurricane will move and what speed its winds will reach.

A watch becomes a warning if a hurricane is expected to hit an area within 24 hours. At this point, people are urged to leave areas where storm surges and flooding are known to occur. Sometimes, emergency officials will issue a mandatory, or required, evacuation of an area. This means everyone must leave right away.

An Uncertain Path

With hurricane forecasts, weather maps often show a cone-shaped path moving across an area. The narrow end of the cone starts at the last-known location of the storm. The cone starts to widen as it travels along the projected path. The farther the forecast goes, the wider—and more uncertain—the storm's path becomes.

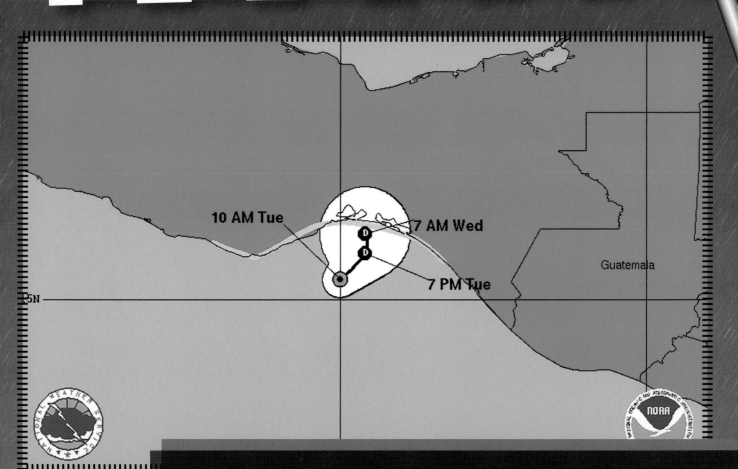

10 AM Tue

7 AM Wed

7 PM Tue

Guatemala

15N

It is impossible to predict a hurricane's path exactly, so weather maps often show a wide area in which the hurricane will most likely make landfall. The path on the map is sometimes called the "cone of uncertainty" or the "cone of concern."

GET READY!

If a meteorologist tells you a hurricane is heading for your area, you need to be prepared. Make sure you have plenty of supplies. Put together an emergency supply kit with items to help you get by for a few days without electricity or running water. Your kit should include bottled water, food that won't spoil, a first-aid kit, medicine, flashlights, a battery-powered radio, and extra batteries. Be sure to have a charged cell phone.

Keep checking news reports about the hurricane as it gets closer. Hurricanes sometimes change course, and it may be safer for you to move to a shelter if your home is suddenly in the storm's direct path.

People often put boards on the windows of their homes or businesses before a hurricane. This may stop the glass from breaking and can also protect the inside of the building from wind and water.

Small but Strong

If the weather forecast calls for a hurricane that's not too big, don't be fooled! Smaller hurricanes can pack a real punch, so you still need to prepare for major storm damage. Hurricane Andrew hit south Florida in 1992 with winds up to 175 miles (281.6 km) per hour, causing severe damage across a strip of land 40 miles (64.4 km) wide.

19

A RISKY CHOICE

People in the path of a hurricane face a big decision: Do they stay in their homes or leave? Sometimes the local government makes that decision. If a hurricane is expected to cause great damage, a mandatory evacuation order may be issued for that area. This means that everyone must leave. These orders protect residents as well as emergency workers.

Some people ignore mandatory evacuation notices. They may not believe the storm will be that bad, or they may have nowhere else to go. But staying in the hurricane's path can be very dangerous, especially because rescuers may not be able to respond to emergency calls in these areas when the hurricane hits.

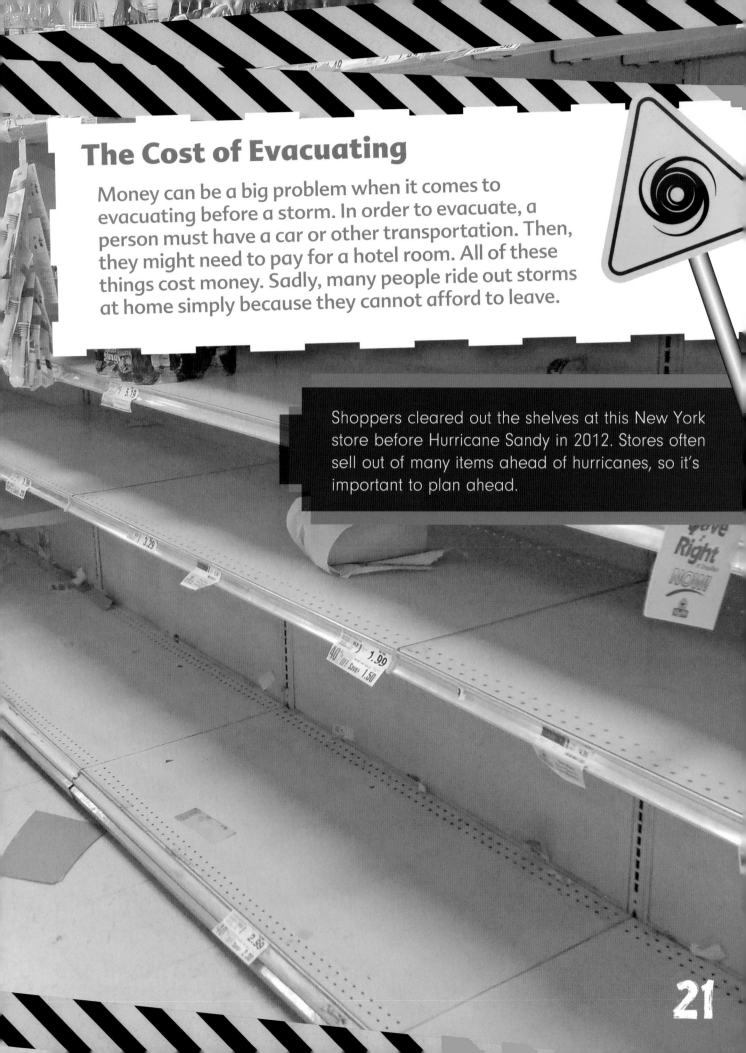

The Cost of Evacuating

Money can be a big problem when it comes to evacuating before a storm. In order to evacuate, a person must have a car or other transportation. Then, they might need to pay for a hotel room. All of these things cost money. Sadly, many people ride out storms at home simply because they cannot afford to leave.

Shoppers cleared out the shelves at this New York store before Hurricane Sandy in 2012. Stores often sell out of many items ahead of hurricanes, so it's important to plan ahead.

WHERE AND WHEN STORMS STRIKE

Hurricanes travel far from where they first form. Storms that affect the United States usually start in the Gulf of Mexico or in the central Atlantic, and sometimes as far away as the western coast of Africa. Coastal states like Florida, Louisiana, North Carolina, and Texas are some of the most commonly hit areas.

The Atlantic hurricane season runs from June 1 until November 30. This is when the greatest number of hurricanes form in this area. The peak of the Atlantic hurricane season is between mid-August and late October. If you plan to travel somewhere tropical during hurricane season, keep an eye on the weather!

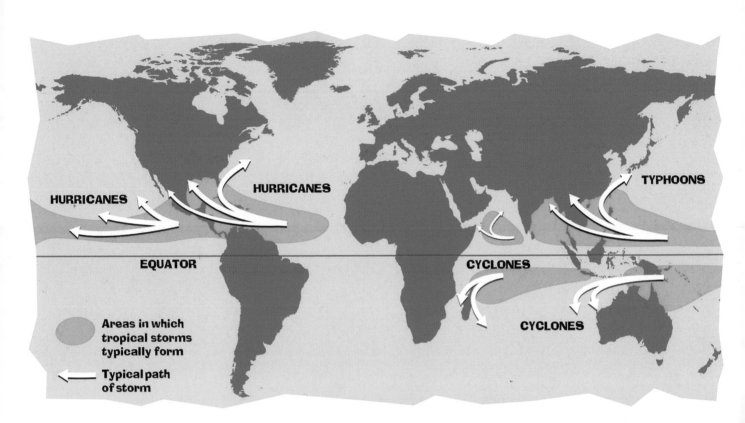

Areas in which tropical storms typically form

Typical path of storm

HURRICANES HURRICANES TYPHOONS

EQUATOR

CYCLONES

CYCLONES

Hurricanes start near the equator. They usually move north and west from there. This is why hurricanes rarely hit West Coast states like California—their path takes them away from the land.

A Long, Dangerous Path

Hurricanes begin to weaken once they are over land. However, this does not mean the storm's threat is over. In 2021, Hurricane Ida made landfall in Louisiana and then traveled more than 1,500 miles (2,414 km) across the United States. The deadly storm caused major flooding and even tornadoes as far away as New Jersey.

EXTREME HURRICANES

The United States has seen some huge hurricanes throughout history. Let's take a look at a few of the most extreme ones.

Deadliest: The Galveston, Texas, hurricane of 1900 killed between 8,000 and 12,000 people. Around 6,000 of these deaths were caused by the 15-foot (4.6-m) storm surge.

Strongest: The Labor Day Hurricane of 1935 was a Category 5 storm. It made landfall in Florida with wind speeds estimated at an incredible 185 miles (298 km) per hour.

Most Costly: Hurricane Katrina struck Louisiana in 2005 as a Category 3 storm. About 1,200 people died, and flooding and high winds caused $161 billion in damages.

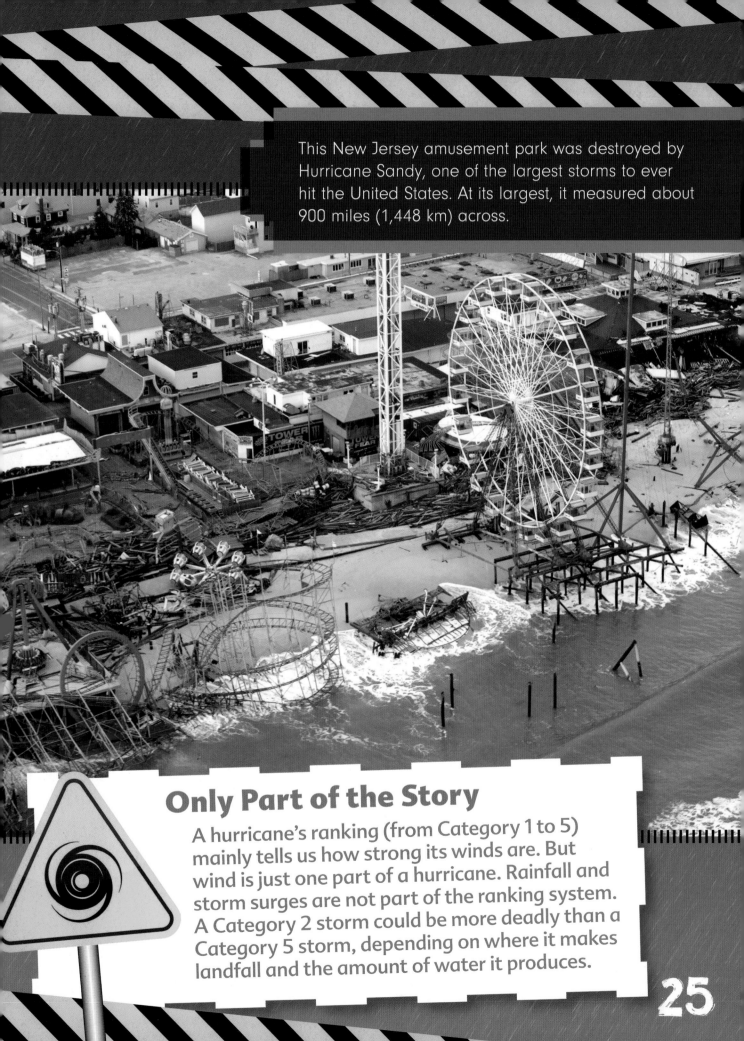

This New Jersey amusement park was destroyed by Hurricane Sandy, one of the largest storms to ever hit the United States. At its largest, it measured about 900 miles (1,448 km) across.

Only Part of the Story

A hurricane's ranking (from Category 1 to 5) mainly tells us how strong its winds are. But wind is just one part of a hurricane. Rainfall and storm surges are not part of the ranking system. A Category 2 storm could be more deadly than a Category 5 storm, depending on where it makes landfall and the amount of water it produces.

THE CLIMATE CHANGE CONNECTION

Scientists believe extreme weather is tied to climate change. Our planet is getting warmer, partly because of things we do every day. This is called global warming. When we drive, cook, or heat our homes, we often use **fossil fuels** like coal and oil. These fuels send gases into the air. The gases trap the sun's heat. Over time, Earth gets warmer.

As the world heats up, so do the oceans. We have more warm water rising into the atmosphere, which makes it easier for hurricanes to form. And with more water in the air, hurricanes will contain even more rain, which could mean lots of large, dangerous storms in the future.

The Greenhouse Effect

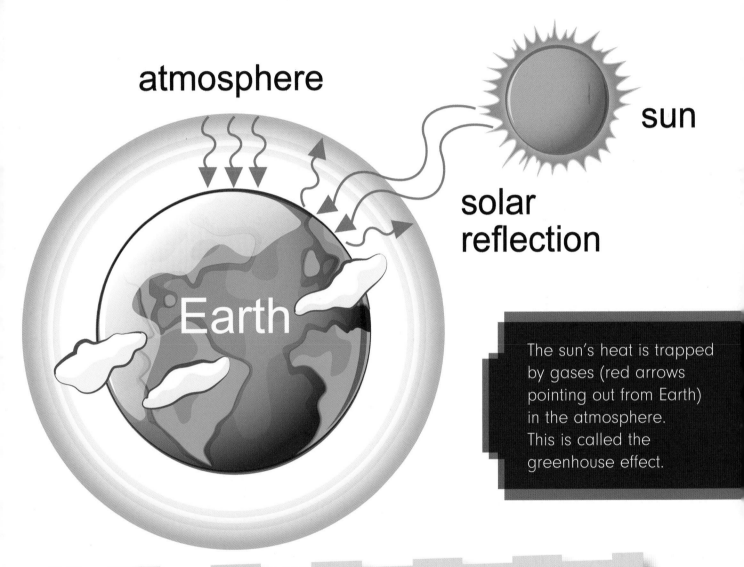

atmosphere

sun

solar
reflection

Earth

The sun's heat is trapped
by gases (red arrows
pointing out from Earth)
in the atmosphere.
This is called the
greenhouse effect.

Global Warming Dangers

Global warming does not just affect the weather.
Warmer temperatures cause snow and ice to
melt. Animals such as polar bears and seals lose
their homes. The melting ice makes the oceans
rise. Higher sea levels cause flooding. They also
harm plants and animals that live in or near
the water.

LOOKING AHEAD

With today's technology, scientists can make more accurate predictions that allow us to prepare for hurricanes. Even so, these dangerous storms can cause serious damage and death. If you live in an area where a hurricane might strike, be smart and safe before the storm arrives.

As our planet continues to change, the weather will change along with it. There is a good chance that extreme weather, like hurricanes, will become more common in the future. People have caused some of the changes that are happening to Earth, but they can also create change for a safer world. Until then, we will be seeing more stormy skies.

How You Can Help

Global warming is a big problem, but even small things can help fix it. Turn off lights when you leave a room. Shut off your computer when you're not using it. Recycle or use less paper. (Trees help the planet by removing harmful gases from the atmosphere.) And spread the word about global warming. Young people can make a big difference when they work together.

In 2017, Hurricane Harvey pounded parts of Texas with 60 inches (152 cm) of rain. Many scientists fear we will see more storms like this one as global warming continues.

GLOSSARY

catastrophic: causing a terrible disaster

damage: harm

equator: an imaginary line around Earth that is the same distance from the North and South Poles

extreme: great or severe

forecast: to make an informed guess about future weather

fossil fuel: matter formed over millions of years from plant and animal remains that is burned for power

intense: existing in an extreme degree

prediction: a guess about what will happen in the future based on facts or knowledge

resident: a person who lives somewhere on a long-term basis

satellite: an object that circles Earth to collect and send information

spiral: a shape or line that curls outward from a center point

tropical: having to do with the warm parts of Earth near the equator

vapor: a substance that is in the form of a gas or contains very small drops mixed with the air

FOR MORE INFORMATION

BOOKS

Gibbons, Gail. *Hurricanes!* New York, NY: Holiday House, 2019.

Jackson, Tom. *How Do We Stop Climate Change?* New York, NY: Earth Aware Editions Kids, 2021.

Tarshis, Lauren. *I Survived the Galveston Hurricane.* New York, NY: Scholastic, 2021.

WEBSITES

Weather Wiz Kids: Hurricanes
www.weatherwizkids.com/weather-hurricane.htm
Check out cool facts about hurricanes and learn some hurricane lingo.

NASA Climate Kids: Weather and Climate
climatekids.nasa.gov/menu/weather-and-climate/
View articles, videos, and photos about weather, climate, and our changing planet.

NOAA SciJinks: How Does a Hurricane Form?
scijinks.gov/hurricane/
Learn more about hurricanes through videos, maps, and illustrations.

INDEX